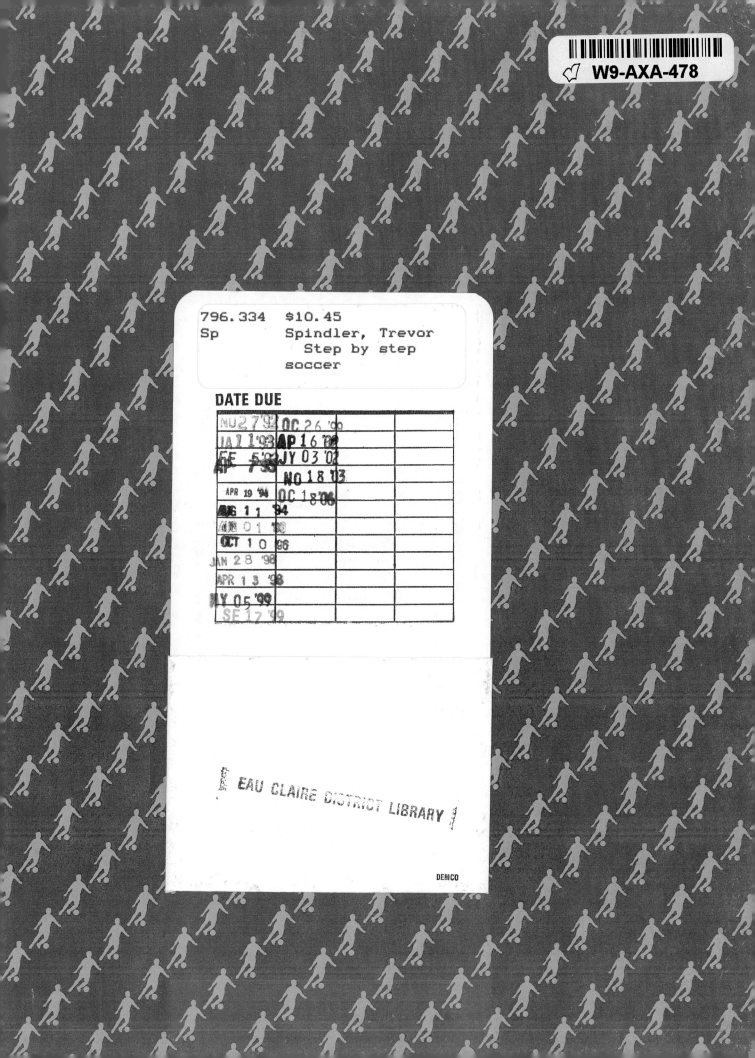

SOCCER

Trevor Spindler and Andrew Ward

GALLERY BOOKS

An Imprint of W.H. Smith Publishers Inc.

112 Madison Avenue
New York City 10016

© **The Automobile Association, 1990**
Fanum House,
Basing View,
Basingstoke RG21 2EA
United Kingdom

ISBN: 0-8317-8053-3

This edition published in 1991 by Gallery Books, an
imprint of W.H. Smith Publishers, Inc., 112 Madison
Avenue, New York, New York 10016

Gallery Books are available for bulk purchase for
sales promotions and premium use. For details write
or telephone the Manager of Special Sales, W.H.
Smith Publishers, Inc., 112 Madison Avenue, New
York, New York 10016. (212) 532-6600

The contents of this book are believed correct at the
time of printing. Nevertheless, the Publishers cannot
accept any responsibility for any errors or omissions
in the details given.

CREDITS

Authors: Trevor Spindler and Andrew Ward
Photography: Allsport Photographic
Illustrations: Oxford Illustrators Ltd.

Typesetting by Microset Graphics Ltd., Basingstoke,
United Kingdom
Color separation by Scantrans Pte Ltd., Singapore
Printed and bound by L.E.G.O. SpA, Italy

The testing methods on pages 68 and 69 were
devised by Robin Russell, and targets for children
(up to 16) can be found in his book *Soccer Star*,
published by the Football Association, 16 Lancaster
Gate, London W2 3LW, England.

Cover and title page: English teams Liverpool and
Norwich in action (Allsport Photographic)

CONTENTS

FOREWORD

Soccer, or association football as it is commonly called, is played in virtually every country in the world. Why is it so popular with so many people?

First, it can be played almost anywhere, on any surface and in most weather conditions. Second, it can be played by adults and children of both sexes. (In the interests of simplicity, the soccer player is referred to as "he" in this book.) Third, all you need to play soccer is a ball of some kind or even a tin can. Whether it is two children playing in the street or two teams battling out the World Cup Final, it is still soccer.

The game of soccer consists of many elements — passing, control, shooting, dribbling, goalkeeping and heading. This variety of techniques makes soccer exciting and enjoyable, but it also makes it challenging. To be a good player you need all-round skills, and the only way to achieve this is by practicing correctly and regularly. This book shows you ways of practicing some of the main aspects of the game. It is very important to practice correctly because what you do in practice you also do in games. It is vital to learn good habits from the start.

To improve your skill, your practice should be progressively more difficult. Start by practicing techniques unopposed, then go on to include teammates and opponents, and finally practice in full-game situations. It is important that you use your weaker foot when practicing, so that you can use it confidently during games. A player who can use only one foot confidently is unlikely to play at a high level.

All the techniques explained in this book can be carried out on your own, or with friends. All you have to do is follow the step-by-step instructions and concentrate on the key points given in each section. These are accompanied by illustrations and color photographs of top-class players in action.

Each topic is given a difficulty rating. First master the techniques with one football player, such as running with the ball, and progress through to the more difficult aspects of the game, denoted by three football players, like the more complicated forms of team tactics. In addition, you have been provided with a STAR TIP in each major section. This will give you an insight into the way professionals think about the game.

Practice is hard work, but improving your performance and developing skillful ways of beating your opponents should also be fun. Players like Englishman Gary Lineker, Argentina's Diego Maradona and Dutchman Ruud Gullit spend many hours practicing. If you do the same, maybe *you* will be a top star one day.

Trevor Spindler

Trevor Spindler

SIMPLY OVERWHELMING
West German supporters in exuberant mood at the 1990 World Cup final in Italy. A crowd of 73,603 people gathered in Rome's Olympic Stadium to watch the West German team play defending champions Argentina.
(Picture: Allsport Photographic/David Cannon)
INSET: Ecstatic West German players Matthäus and Littbarski celebrate their 1-0 victory over Argentina in the 1990 World Cup final. The winning goal was scored by Andreas Brehme from the penalty spot, with only five minutes to go before the end of the match.
(Picture: Allsport Photographic)

INTRODUCTION

Soccer has a long history. In the sport's early days, players worked as *individuals*, running with the ball as far as they could, hoping that a teammate would take up the running after they lost control of the ball. In those days players rarely headed the ball, and goalkeepers were too unprotected to risk catching the ball too often.

Then came the passing game. Let the ball do the work, someone said. Heading, tackling, intercepting and goalkeeping all became specialized skills. In the 1900s a Scottish international goalkeeper discovered scientific techniques of narrowing the angle of a player's shot, while two English defenders developed the offside tactic, whereby opponents were *put* offside on purpose.

After this time, team tactics became important and the sport increased in its scope. The European Championship and the World Cup gave soccer more importance. And the spread of soccer in the United States has given the sport a world stage.

Not only is soccer played worldwide, but it is a sport that can appeal to all types of people — old and young, men and women. It has been played by

The penalty area is where the goalkeeper can handle the ball. It is also where an offense by the defending team can merit a penalty kick. The two goals, each 8 yards (7.32m) wide and 8ft (2.44m) high, are marked by posts (not more than 5in (12cm) wide) and a crossbar. The object of the game is to score more goals than the opposition.

THE FIELD OF PLAY
Soccer's rectangular field is marked with distinctive lines (see diagram) which are not more than 5in (12cm) wide. Each corner has a flagpost at least 5ft (1.5m) high. Flagposts may also be placed at the halfway line, 1 yard (1m) outside the field of play.

At the center of the field is a circle with a radius of 10 yards (9.15m). Players should be at least 10 yards (9.15m) from the ball when opponents take a place kick (or any free kick). The penalty area arc helps the

referee assess if players are this distance from a penalty kick.

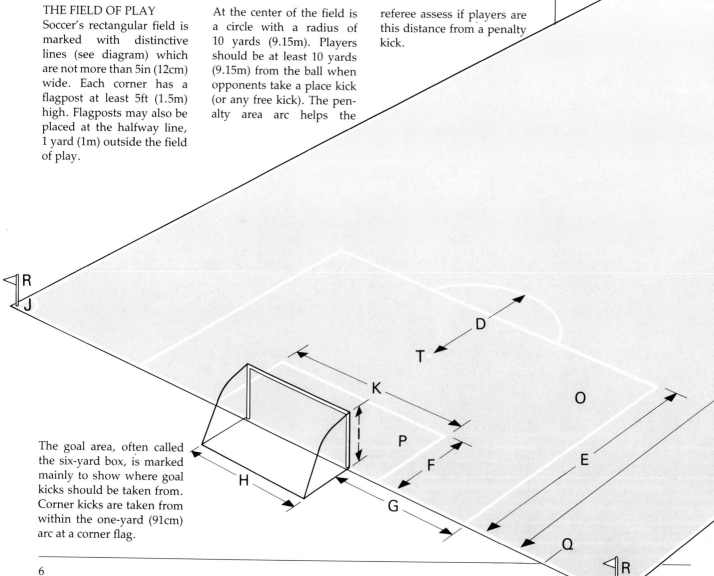

The goal area, often called the six-yard box, is marked mainly to show where goal kicks should be taken from. Corner kicks are taken from within the one-yard (91cm) arc at a corner flag.

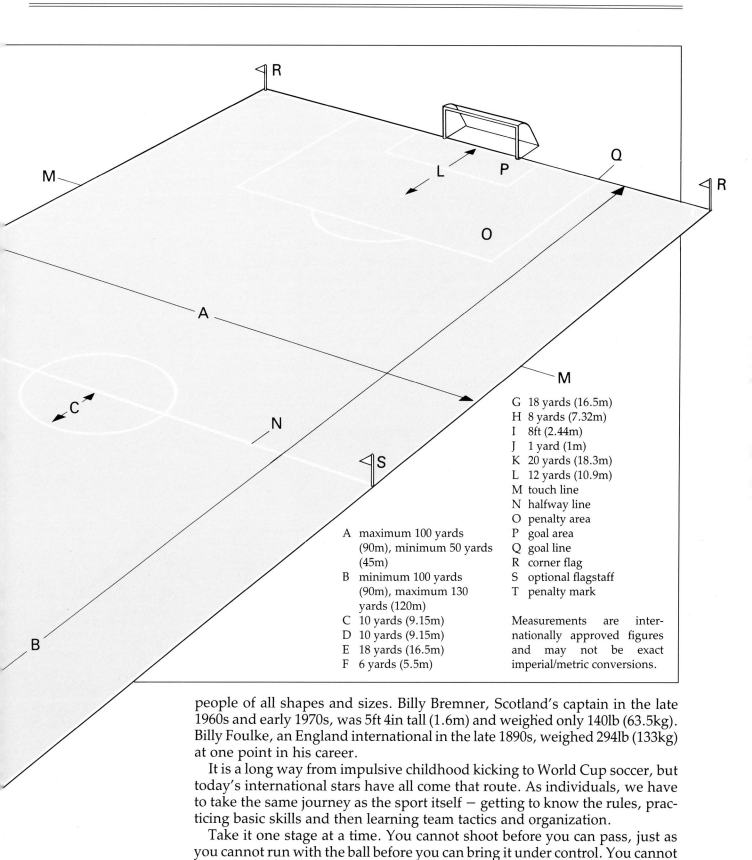

G 18 yards (16.5m)
H 8 yards (7.32m)
I 8ft (2.44m)
J 1 yard (1m)
K 20 yards (18.3m)
L 12 yards (10.9m)
M touch line
N halfway line
O penalty area
P goal area
Q goal line
R corner flag
S optional flagstaff
T penalty mark

A maximum 100 yards
   (90m), minimum 50 yards
   (45m)
B minimum 100 yards
   (90m), maximum 130
   yards (120m)
C 10 yards (9.15m)
D 10 yards (9.15m)
E 18 yards (16.5m)
F 6 yards (5.5m)

Measurements are internationally approved figures and may not be exact imperial/metric conversions.

people of all shapes and sizes. Billy Bremner, Scotland's captain in the late 1960s and early 1970s, was 5ft 4in tall (1.6m) and weighed only 140lb (63.5kg). Billy Foulke, an England international in the late 1890s, weighed 294lb (133kg) at one point in his career.

It is a long way from impulsive childhood kicking to World Cup soccer, but today's international stars have all come that route. As individuals, we have to take the same journey as the sport itself — getting to know the rules, practicing basic skills and then learning team tactics and organization.

Take it one stage at a time. You cannot shoot before you can pass, just as you cannot run with the ball before you can bring it under control. You cannot score the winning goal in a World Cup Final until you know about soccer.

EQUIPMENT AND CLOTHING

As part of a team, a soccer player often has little choice about equipment. Shirts, shorts and socks should all be uniform in pattern, color and material, so try not to be too fussy about these items. It is no use saying, "Blue doesn't suit me. Can I play in red?"

In some small details of equipment, such as shoes and shinpads, you can choose what is most comfortable for *you*. Players are notoriously particular about their shoes. Goalkeepers have special requirements and may be the fashion pacesetters of a team.

Usually you will have no choice over the ball, which must weigh 14 to 16 oz (396-453g) and should keep its shape. It is acceptable to practice with balls of differing weights and sizes — tennis balls can help develop ball control — but remember that senior soccer games take place with a full size ball. Until age 16, however, a slightly smaller ball is recommended. Remember to wipe your soccer ball after use, and let it down slightly if you will not be using it for some time.

FOOTWEAR
The two main types of soccer shoes are the molded-sole shoe — for hard, dry playing fields — and the screw-in cleat shoe for softer surfaces. The screw-in feature allows you to vary the length of studs. Try to test your footwear on the field before a game to assess what is comfortable for the day's conditions.

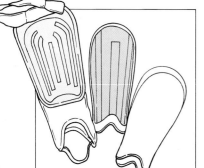

SHINPADS
Most top coaches demand that their players wear shinpads between the sock and skin to protect legs from knocks and bruises. Some pads have built-in ankle protectors. If yours haven't, push a wad of cotton padding inside the sock around the ankle instead. Shinpads will not slow you down. You will soon hardly notice you are wearing them.

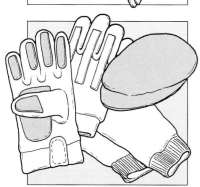

GOALKEEPER'S EQUIPMENT
Wear a distinctively colored jersey, having checked the opposition's colors. Take onto the field a pair of gloves (useful in wet weather) and a hat with a brim (to keep the sun from your eyes). Keep these in the back of your net when not using them. For hard playing fields you may need good-quality equipment, such as padded shorts and shirt. In frosty conditions you may wish to consider knee protection.

GOALKEEPER'S EQUIPMENT
Swedish international Thomas Ravelli is wearing the traditional goalkeeping color of green throughout, even though the rest of the Swedish players will be wearing blue shorts and yellow socks. Ravelli has modern-style goalkeeping gloves.

INSET: Bulgarian goalkeeper Mikhailov (in yellow) is shown in an ungainly pose as he concedes a goal to Valdano of Argentina. The bag in the net is for Mikhailov's accessories.

 STAR TIP
If you are tying up your socks to stop them coming down, make sure they can be adjusted quickly or easily removed, should you be injured. A wide strip of any material except elastic will do. Turn the knot to the side of the sock so that it doesn't cut into the bone at the front. A second tie-up can be used on the outside of the sock below the shinpad.

PASSING THE BALL (1)

When kicking or passing the ball, different parts of the foot are used for different purposes — the instep for power, the inside of the foot for accuracy, the outside of the foot for swerve or disguise. Kicking the ball is something players can practice, either on their own or with others. Start with the ball stationary, but quickly go on to kicking a moving ball because that is what you will have to do in a game.

You will see from the techniques below that there are certain themes to passing correctly. Try to keep your head steady and eyes on the ball. Place *both* feet in the correct position for the technique and strike the appropriate part of the ball for the particular pass. The stronger and straighter the follow-through, the greater the power and accuracy.

THE PUSH PASS

The inside of the foot is best for pushing the ball a short distance. A "pendulum" action is used. The key factors are:
- head steady and eyes on the ball;
- nonkicking foot alongside the ball and pointing in the direction of the pass;
- kicking foot turned out and ankle firm;
- contact with the midline of ball;
- follow through with a high knee in the line of the kick (not across the body).

THE LOW DRIVE

The instep, that part of the foot under the shoelace, is mostly used for power, such as for shooting. The key factors are:
- head steady and eyes on the ball;
- nonkicking foot alongside the ball;
- ankle firm, toes pointed downwards;
- contact through the midline of the ball to keep the ball down;
- follow through with a full swing of the leg after kicking the ball.

THE LOFTED PASS

This is for long-distance passing over opponents. One method uses the instep and a wide approach to the ball (about 45 degrees):
- head steady, eyes on the ball;
- nonkicking foot 12-18in (30-45cm) to the side of the ball and behind it;
- ankle firm, toes pointed out;
- body leaning back;
- contact through the ball's bottom half;
- follow through with a full leg swing.

PASSING AND KICKING
Kim Sang Ho of South Korea demonstrates some of the key factors of passing and kicking. Notice how his head is steady, his eyes are on the ball, and the nonkicking foot (his right) is wide of the ball and behind it in order to make a lofted pass. Having prepared for the pass by drawing back his left foot, he will now swing it through the ball.

 STAR TIP
Practice kicking the ball with both feet. Most of us prefer either our right or left foot, but the best players can use both. To be the best you will have to practice with your weaker foot.

PASSING THE BALL (2)

1 In this first picture the player runs towards a stationary ball in preparation for a low drive. At this point, he has already assessed the position of the other players, including the goalkeeper if this is a shot at goal. Notice how his head is steady and his eyes are now concentrating on the ball rather than the other players. He is taking a fairly straight approach to the ball, and his left arm is outstretched for balance.

2 His approach to the ball is now almost complete and he is taking a good position for the low drive. His nonkicking foot, in this case the left, is close to the ball. His head remains steady and his eyes are still on the ball. His right ankle is firm and his toes are pointed down. His right leg is drawn back, bent at the knee. He is ready to straighten the leg, and it is this straightening action that will provide the power for the kick.

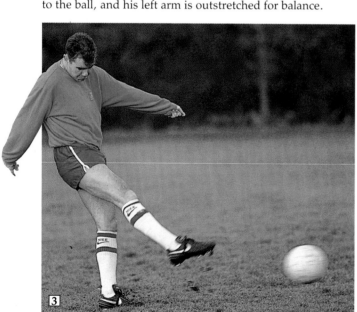

3 With his head in an excellent position, steady and down over the ball, the player has straightened his leg to kick through the ball, striking it around the midline to keep a fairly low trajectory. His arms are now both outstretched to give him balance.

4 The fourth picture of the sequence shows our player following through with his kick. The waist-high follow-through will improve the kick, and the follow-through should be in the direction of the shot or pass. The ball is on its way towards the target, and the player's head is now, and only now, coming up to see what is happening to the ball.

5 The final picture of the sequence shows the player airborne after a low drive. The power of his follow-through has taken him into the air, his arms still outstretched to maintain balance. His right foot is returning to the ground, but his left still has a spring from the power generated. His eyes now concentrate on as much of the field as they can.

6 – 7 This two-picture sequence shows how the approach to the ball is different for making a lofted pass. This first picture shows the player running from an angle of about 45 degrees, a perfect angle for the lofted pass.

7 Rather than place his nonkicking foot (his left) close to and alongside the ball, the kicker has placed it slightly behind the ball and about 18 in (45 cm) away. With kicking foot raised, knee bent, head steady and eyes on the ball, he is now perfectly positioned for a lofted pass.

PASSING THE BALL (3)

Even stars like Diego Maradona and Ruud Gullit practice kicking technique, especially after a lay-off through injury or vacation. You should never feel above practicing passing. All you need is a ball and somebody to kick it to. If you're on your own, then use a wall.

The art of chipping and volleying the ball takes time to master. Marco van Basten's famous volley for Holland against the Soviet Union in the 1988 European Championship Final was not simply a spur-of-the-moment decision. It was the result of years of practice.

There are various techniques for volleying. It depends on whether the ball is coming from the side or the front, and whether you are attacking or defending. A volley at goal will need the ball kept low, but a defender will volley the ball below its midline in order to gain height on the clearance.

OVERHEAD KICK
Scotland's Maurice Johnston scores with an overhead volley against Cyprus in a World Cup qualifying game. This advanced skill takes place without a good sighting of the target, in this case the goal. Notice how Johnston lets his body fall away, which is essential with all volleying. The higher the ball, the more you must fall away if you are to keep the ball down.

 STAR TIP

Volleying is a difficult skill, but to beat your opponent to the ball you sometimes have to take the ball when it is still in the air. When volleying, relax and go for contact with the ball rather than thinking about power. If your timing is good, you will put pace on the ball without needing too much extra strength.

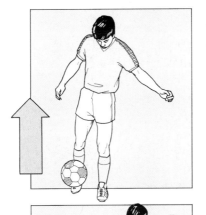

CHIPPING THE BALL

When faced with a line of defenders, one way forward is over the top. This needs a technique to gain height over a short distance, putting backspin on the ball so it doesn't overrun:

- head steady and eyes on the ball;
- nonkicking foot at the side of the ball;
- a straight approach;
- use the instep on the ball's lowest part;
- stab the ball with little follow-through.

THE FLICK PASS

Kicking with the outside of the foot is useful over short distances, especially if tightly marked. The key factors are:

- head steady and eyes on the ball;
- nonkicking foot behind and to the side of the ball;
- kicking foot inside the line of the ball;
- quick rotation of the foot outwards;
- contact the midline of the ball with little follow-through.

VOLLEYING THE BALL

The ball is volleyed when a dropping ball is kicked before it touches the ground. The key points for an attacking volley *from the side* are:

- head steady and eyes on the ball;
- ankle firm and extended;
- nonkicking foot to the side of the ball;
- kicking leg swings around and across the body;
- contact through the ball's midline.

CONTROLLING THE BALL

To be a good player, you must be able to control the ball. Good control gives you time and space to pass, dribble or shoot.

Any part of the body can be used to control the ball (except hands and arms). No matter which way you choose to control the ball, or whichever part of the body you use, there are three key principles involved:

(1) Keep your head steady and watch the ball carefully;

(2) Move into the line of the ball;

(3) Decide which part of the body to use.

If you have plenty of space, you may decide to use "cushion control" so that the ball drops close to you. If an opponent is nearby, you may decide on "firm control" so the ball runs away from him.

ONE-TOUCH CONTROL

Ray Houghton, of top English team Liverpool and the Republic of Ireland (Eire), moves in to control the ball. Although the ball is at an awkward height, Houghton will have it under control in a split second.

INSET: Steve Staunton, Houghton's club and international colleague, keeps his head steady and watches the ball carefully as he moves to control it with his chest.

 STAR TIP

The ball is brought under control to do one of three things — pass, dribble or shoot. Whatever you decide to do, it should be done as soon as the ball is under control. If you are not quick, your opponent will be across to mark you closely and you will lose the time and space that was available at first.

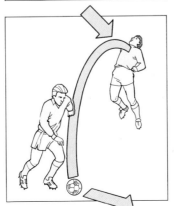

CUSHION CONTROL

The aim of cushion control is to take nearly all the pace out of the ball. First, remember the three principles of controlling the ball (see above). Then consider two others:

- offer the key part of your body to the ball;
- as the ball hits you, withdraw the surface and relax to take the pace from the ball, allowing it to drop in front of you. When cushioning with chest and head, bend your legs on impact.

FIRM CONTROL

During a game the ball often comes to you when there is an opponent nearby. To give yourself as much time as possible in this situation, you should control the ball so that it runs away from your opponent. Remember the three principles for controlling the ball (see above), and then consider two further points:

- *partly* relax the controlling surface to keep some pace on the ball;
- at the moment of impact, turn the surface so that you are forcing the ball in the direction you want to go.

ONE-TOUCH CONTROL

Practice will help you control a ball at any height, whether using your feet, thigh, chest or head. Aim to control the ball with your first touch and pass, dribble or shoot with your second. If you can do this, opponents will not have time to challenge you.

HEADING THE BALL (1)

Few players are as confident when the ball is in the air as when it is on the ground. They may worry about colliding with other players or suffering headaches from heading the ball wrongly. A few simple points will set these worries aside.

Heading is an essential part of soccer, and you don't have to be very tall to benefit from the skill. Many brilliant headers of the ball have been comparatively small players. When the ball is in the air, remember that almost anybody can run 5 to 10 yards (4.5-9m) during the time it takes for the ball to arrive. Tell yourself that it can be you.

Start learning heading techniques by heading the ball from your hands as you hold it in front of you. When you have mastered this, stand still and head the ball after it has been gently thrown in the air. Once you are confident about how to head (see below), go on to the two main types of heading — heading in defense and heading in attack.

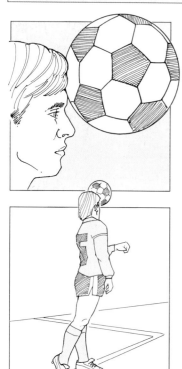

HOW TO HEAD
Watch the ball with both eyes open until the moment your head makes contact. Use the forehead, which is well-protected by bone. (Most people take the ball too high on their head, a cause of headaches.) Use firm neck muscles for power, transfer your weight through the ball and make contact with the correct part of the ball, depending on where you are directing your header.

HEADING IN DEFENSE
In and around your own penalty area, try to achieve:
height on the ball, to give your team time;
distance on your header, to take the ball as far as possible from goal;
width, to take the ball towards the wing.

Follow the basic principles of how to head (above) but head below the ball's midline to direct it upwards. Don't head the bottom of the ball or it will go straight up.

HEADING IN ATTACK
When heading towards goal, aim low rather than high. A goalkeeper will always have more difficulty reaching a ground ball than one at a comfortable height within arm's reach. Follow the basic principles of how to head (above) but head through the midline of the ball or just above it.

*HEADING IN
A GAME
Andrea Carnavale of Italy outjumps two Brazilian players.
INSET: Gordon Durie of Scotland has anticipated the path of the ball and slipped into some space in the penalty area to head a goal against Yugoslavia in a World Cup qualifying tie. Despite the excitement of the situation, Durie is calmly following the basic principles of heading, keeping his eye on the ball and watching it onto his forehead.*

 *STAR
TIP
Much of the secret of heading comes from getting into the right position to make a header. This usually means getting in front of or away from opponents, making certain you get to the ball first. It means anticipating where the ball is going to be played. If you are not in a clear position to head for goal, head towards a colleague who is better placed.*

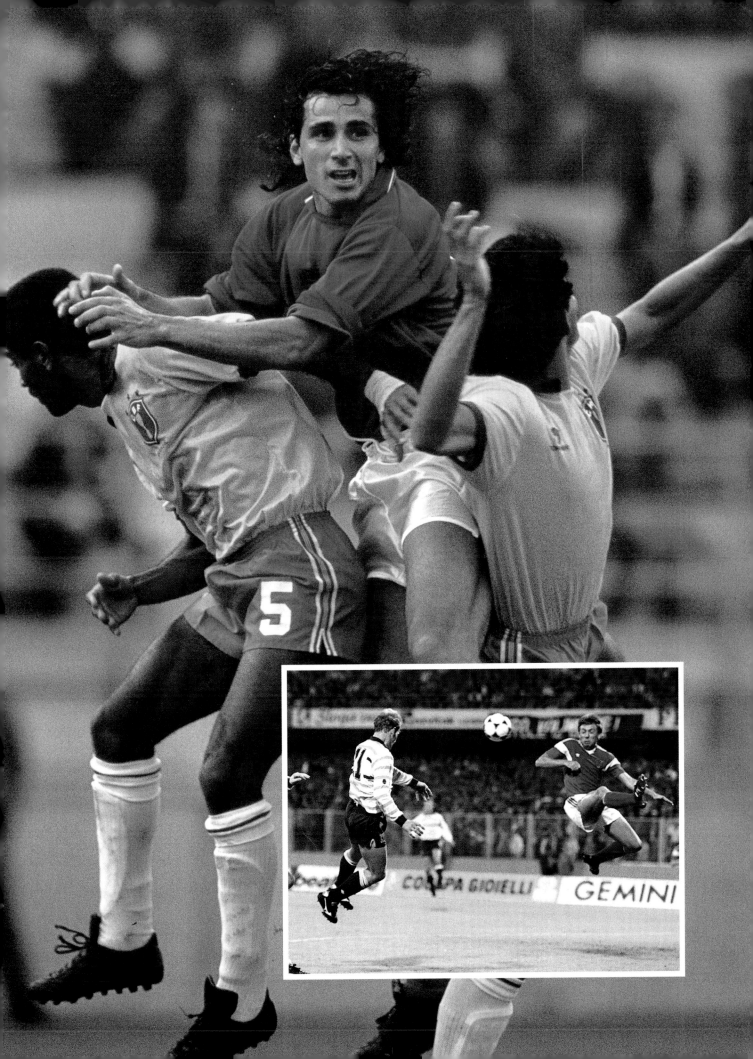

HEADING THE BALL (2)

Some top-class defenders can head the ball almost as far as they can kick it. Some top-class attackers claim they can direct the ball more accurately when it is in the air than on the ground.

Although most of the game is played with the feet, a header often provides the most dramatic turning point of a game. Most post-war World Cup Finals have included headed goals, such as those of Pele for Brazil in 1958 and 1970, Geoff Hurst for England against West Germany in 1966, Nanninga for Holland against Argentina in 1978 and Jose Luis Brown for Argentina against West Germany in 1986. Yet, if you read these notes carefully, you will realize that much of heading is to do with using your feet properly, running into position and jumping correctly. Think about your heading and where you are heading the ball to.

HEADING WITH POWER

In general, the faster you are moving when you head the ball, the harder you will head it. Tensing neck muscles also helps. If you have your feet on the ground, keep them well apart so you can move your shoulders back and bring them forward again as you strike the ball. If you are in the air, arch your back, then bend at the waist. Raise your arms as you take off.

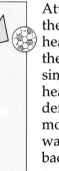

DEFLECTING THE BALL

Attackers, anxious for surprise, often use the tactic of deflecting the ball with the head rather than heading in the direction they are facing. The principles are very similar – keep your eye on the ball and head the ball with your forehead. For deflecting sideways, turn your head at the moment of impact. For deflecting backwards, a more advanced skill, arch your back and move your head back at the moment of impact.

TIMING YOUR RUN AND JUMP

Jump from one foot, taking a long final stride with the body leaning back, a little like a high jumper. Attacking the ball means that it will jar you less on impact. The secret is to try to meet the ball at the highest point you can comfortably reach. Practice is essential. You may be able to add an extra inch or two to the height of your jump, and that could win or save you a game.

ATTACKING THE BALL
Sauzee of France shows the benefit of attacking the ball in this photograph, taken immediately after he has headed clear from Ally McCoist of Scotland. Sauzee has jumped incredibly high and has put height and distance on his clearance. The thrust from his torso and neck muscles add to the distance he will achieve with this powerful header.

 STAR TIP

It is no good going through all the effort of running, jumping and heading the ball if the final outcome of your header is off target or straight to an opponent, yet this commonly happens, even at the highest level. Develop a sense for where the goal and the players are, while keeping your eyes on the ball to head it.

"With the ball apparently tied to his laces he darted through the heart of the England defense, glided between two defenders, beyond a third and held off yet another as he deceived Shilton to slide the ball home."

This is *World Soccer's* description of Diego Maradona's second goal for Argentina against England in the quarter-final of the 1986 World Cup Finals. To many spectators, there is still nothing more exciting than a player taking on a number of defenders on his own. How does he do it? Why does it look so easy?

He does it by developing good control of the ball, strength at holding off players, deception to throw them off balance and speed over short distances, perhaps 5 or 10 yards (4.5-9m). Above all, good dribbling, or footwork, requires an excellent sense of balance and the ability to sway and change direction without falling over. It is something players can practice on their own (see the exercises on pages 68 and 69).

CLOSE CONTROL ACTION

England's Gary Lineker, with the ball in close control, has lured a Polish defender into an attempt to take the ball before deceiving him with a change of direction. The defender is not only off balance but on the floor, which means he will be out of the game for vital seconds while recovering. Lineker is ready to step up his pace and continue the attack.

 STAR TIP

It is important to choose the best time to dribble and the best time to pass. It is also important to dribble in positions which offer your team the highest reward, such as near your opponents' penalty area. Don't dribble near your own penalty area, where it is very dangerous if you lose the ball.

CLOSE CONTROL

When dribbling, a player should start with the ball under control within a comfortable distance of the feet, close enough to allow a quick change of direction without having to retrieve the ball first.

CHANGE OF DIRECTION

When dribbling, the player aims to retain his own balance while throwing defenders off balance. Opponents can be thrown off balance by simple deceptive movements, such as swaying the body one way and moving the ball in the other direction, or taking it one way with the feet and moving it swiftly back in the other direction. Practice is important here, as is watching the movements of star players. Remember that a two-footed player will always have scope when dribbling and can move the ball from foot to foot to tease defenders.

CHANGE OF PACE

Once you have thrown your opponent off balance, you must accelerate away before he recovers. It is best to push the ball behind the defender to force him to turn before chasing you, but make sure you keep the ball away from other opponents. Your speed over a few yards is crucial. If you get clear you may wish to run further with the ball. This needs a special technique (see pages 24 and 25).

RUNNING WITH THE BALL

Running with the ball is not the same as dribbling. When you dribble, you try to beat opponents. When you run with the ball, you take it across spaces where there are no opponents.

The idea is to move as quickly as possible away from opponents who are in pursuit. Not surprisingly, this is usually more common in attack than defense, but all players will, sooner or later, find themselves in the clear, if only for 10 or 15 yards (9-14m). This may happen in all sorts of ways: you may dribble past an opponent into space; a failed interception may mean the ball comes through to you; or a through-ball may be directed into your path.

Study the tips below and improve your speed at this important technique. It may seem exciting to be given a 5-yard (4.5m) start over the defense at the halfway line, but only the best ball runners are capable of holding that advantage and retaining their technique for a shot at goal.

LOOKING UP
Ruud Gullit, the brilliant Dutch star, is pictured a split second after he has touched the ball forward. He is now using the time before his next touch to look up and decide his next move. Gullit's flowing hair and long stride are evidence that he is building up a quick pace. He knows he will have to compete with players who are sprinting without the ball.
INSET: José Cuciuffo of Argentina.

 STAR TIP
Running quickly with the ball is vital because it creates the time for your next move, but whichever move you choose — a pass, a dribble or a shot — it will be more difficult to execute it at speed than when stationary. Steady yourself as you reach the ball at the end of your run and make sure your head is down.

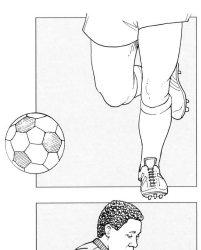

BALL IN FRONT
You can't run quickly if the ball is under your feet. Push it firmly ahead of you. The more quickly you are running, the further you can push it, but make sure an opponent can't reach it. There is no specific distance that you should push the ball. This depends on where the opponents are. A good rule of thumb is that if you push the ball more than halfway to an opponent, the opponent should reach the ball before you. This also applies to goalkeepers in a one-against-one break on goal.

HEAD UP
As you chase the ball, run straight and look up so you can see where your teammates and opponents are. At all times of a game you should know where the other players are. This will help you decide what you ought to do with the ball — pass, dribble or shoot. But remember that you will need to look at the ball each time you touch it forward.

USE YOUR LACES
Kick the ball with your laces so that you don't have to slow down every time you touch it. The aim of running with the ball is to be able to take each touch in your stride, so that you don't lose the pace you have built up. If you touch the ball too often, your pace will be slowed.

TURNING WITH THE BALL

THE MAN-TO-MAN DEFENDER

If you have your back to goal and are tightly covered, you are little danger to the opposition. In this situation, players who can escape their defender and turn with the ball are valuable members of their team. The basic technique for turning is to change direction quickly and take the ball with you, and here are three techniques for achieving that aim. The starting position, shown here, is with your back to goal and tightly covered.

1 FIRST TECHNIQUE

The first technique is to use the inside of the foot to reach out and bring the ball back across your body. Try to keep your body between the opponent and the ball, preventing the defender from both seeing and reaching the ball. By changing the direction of the ball, your opponent will be thrown off balance. A two-footed player will obviously have the option of turning to the right or the left with this technique, and this should keep the defender in two minds.

2 Once you have turned quickly and thrown the player off balance, be ready to move forward and attack swiftly with a pass, a dribble or a shot. As with the technique of dribbling, try to change your speed and move away quickly. This will make it more difficult for your opponent to recover.

3 SECOND TECHNIQUE
A second technique for turning is to use the outside of the foot. Having started from the same position as the first diagram — back to goal and tightly covered — use the outside of the foot to reach out and bring the ball back across your body. It is important to get the foot round the ball. Pivot on the other foot and move off in the opposite direction.

4 THIRD TECHNIQUE
A third technique, the drag-back, is useful if your opponent is in a position alongside you, tightly covering you and preventing you from making an easy turn towards goal. If the defender is threatening to get around the front of you, and there is space behind you, then set yourself up for the drag-back by positioning yourself so the ball can be played by the foot furthest from the opponent.

5 Then, as you move forward into the ball, reach out and drag it back by rolling the sole of your foot across the top of the ball. Pivot on the other foot and move away in the other direction. Again, this should provide you with space to make a quick decision about your next move — a pass, a dribble or a shot.

ON THE BALL

[1] On the ball in this sequence is Trevor Francis, whose 20-year top-level playing career has lasted throughout the 1970s and 1980s. Francis, who played for England on 52 occasions, played around the world with Birmingham City, Detroit Express, Nottingham Forest, Manchester City, Sampdoria, Glasgow Rangers, Queen's Park Rangers and Sheffield Wednesday. His particular qualities of speed and ball control in and around the opponents' penalty area made him the subject of the first £1 million transfer between English clubs. Here Francis, wearing the red shirt of Nottingham Forest, has the ball at his feet just outside the penalty area but has his back to goal. The Norwich City defender (yellow shirt) has taken a good covering position.

[2] Francis has swayed sharply to his right while retaining his balance and ability to move in either direction. The defender behind him senses he can take the ball, while a supporting defender (extreme left) has covered Francis's chance of passing to a colleague. Notice how Francis's move to the right has committed the defender to attempt to take the ball with his right foot. Notice also that four other Norwich City players have taken up covering positions. The odds seem overwhelmingly in favor of the defending team.

[3] Having first swayed to the right, Francis now turns the ball to his left with the outside of his left foot. He has thrown the defender off balance and forced him to

mistime his attempt. Francis has also played the ball into a position that suits him for his next move.

4 Although slightly off balance himself, Francis keeps his body low to aid his turning and begins to regain his balance as quickly as possible. At this point, the defender has recovered some ground, but Francis has deliberately played the ball a little wider of the goal and has the ball under some control.

5 Francis is now on the move and is running almost directly towards goal. For the second time, the defender senses danger and believes he can take the ball. He slides across to make a risky challenge right on the edge of the penalty area.

6 Again, Francis is too quick for him. He has flicked the ball away from the defender with his left foot and is now finding time to look out of the corner of his eye at the other players and the goal. He wants to know where he has players in support and where the defenders are. Will he attempt to dribble past the next challenge? Will he try a shot? Or will he try to pass to the colleague who is moving into a position in the center of the penalty area?

SHOOTING

The quality of shooting frequently decides the result of a game. One team may create 20 scoring opportunities and not take advantage of any of them, while their opponents may take the one chance they create. If you want to make the best of your scoring chances, you must practice shooting. Practice with dropping and bouncing balls because that is what you can expect in a game.

Shooting covers a variety of kicking and passing techniques. Indeed, when you are shooting you are "passing the ball into goal." Which technique you use will depend on how and where the shooting opportunity occurs. Therefore you must practice *all* the passing techniques explained on pages 10 to 15, and you must be able to use both feet.

The main shooting considerations are accuracy and power.

POSITIVE ATTACK
England's Steve Bull attacks a bouncing ball positively. He knows the goalkeeper's position and has committed himself to a powerful drive with a part of the goal to aim at. His head is steady and his eyes watch the ball.
INSET: West Germany's Jürgen Klinsmann celebrates the outcome of good shooting — a goal against Denmark.

STAR TIP
Just before you shoot, if you have time, look up and check the position of the goalkeeper. This will help you decide where to shoot and how to shoot. If the goalkeeper has committed himself or is badly positioned, you may be able to take advantage of this. Make up your mind quickly and then concentrate on your shooting technique.

ACCURACY
When you shoot, force the opposition's goalkeeper to make a save rather than give him the luxury of watching the ball go wide of goal or over the top. During a game, too many shots miss the target. At least if a ball is going wide someone may deflect the ball into goal, but nobody can reach a ball going over the crossbar. Strike the ball cleanly and keep it low.

POWER
Once your shooting is accurate, you should try to increase its power. Powerful shots are more difficult for the goalkeeper to hold. Driving (page 10) and volleying (page 15) are appropriate techniques for power. The more power you use, the more likely it is that the ball will rise over the crossbar, so keep your head down and strike through the midline of the ball or just above it.

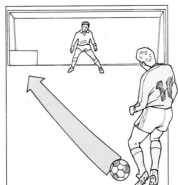

WHERE TO SHOOT
Which part of the goal you aim for will depend on the positioning of other players, especially the goalkeeper. When the goalkeeper is well positioned, you should aim *low* and to the *far post*. Low shots are much more difficult to save because the goalkeeper has to drop down. Shots to the far post are more difficult to deflect out of play, and teammates following up may be able to score from the rebound.

GOALKEEPING (1)

It is often said that goalkeepers must be crazy. One former England international goalkeeper, while agreeing with this remark, commented that it wasn't goalkeeping that drove him crazy but watching his forwards try to score goals.

A goalkeeper is the odd one out in a soccer team — the only one allowed to handle the ball (although only in his team's penalty area) and the only one who can see all his team's play in front of him. These oddities mean that a goalkeeper must have special skills and recognize that he has a unique role as the last line of defense.

When choosing a goalkeeper, a coach will look for courage, confidence, agility, strength and anticipation. A knowledge of other positions may help, as goalkeepers need to read the minds of opponents. What is also crucial, though, is the goalkeeper's ability to learn the key skills. This first section deals with situations which show clearly the value of the first rule of goalkeeping — whenever you can, get your body behind the ball to give you a second line of defense.

STARTING POSITION
When about to receive the ball, there are four factors to remember:
- head steady and eyes on the ball;
- the feet should be a shoulder-width apart and the body weight is forward;
- forearms should be waist high and outside the body;
- palms should be towards the ball.

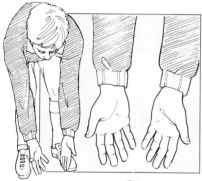

THE STOOP TECHNIQUE
This technique for saving shots near your feet involves several key points:
- a sidestepping movement to get in line with the shot;
- feet fairly close together;
- head steady and eyes on the ball;
- bend at the waist;
- palms upwards, little fingers together;
- scoop the ball to your chest.

THE KNEELING TECHNIQUE
A second technique for saving nearby ground shots is the kneeling technique:
- sidestep into the line of the ball;
- feet sideways on to the path of the ball;
- place one knee close to the other foot;
- turn your chest towards the ball;
- head steady, eyes on the ball;
- palms upwards, little fingers together;
- scoop the ball to your chest.

MOVING INTO POSITION
The goalkeeper moving into the "starting position" is Walter Zenga of Italy. Notice how his body weight is shifting forward and his eyes are concentrating hard on the play. INSET: Jozsef Szendrei of Hungary shows the importance of getting the body behind the ball when making a save. Szendrei focuses on the ball despite the presence of Holland's Ruud Gullit.

 STAR TIP
Be prepared to adapt your technique for saving ground shots if the ball is bouncing unpredictably along the ground. Your bent knee may need to be a few inches off the ground to make sure more of your body is behind the ball. Make sure you avoid every goalkeeper's nightmare — letting the ball pass between your legs.

GOALKEEPING (2)

Goalkeepers are often remembered for embarrassing mistakes rather than spectacular saves, so they should practice basic catching techniques regularly. When the ball is in the air, goalkeepers have a big advantage over other players — they can use their hands to control the ball.

Catching the ball is really another form of cushion control (see page 17), except that the control surface is the hands. Sometimes, if a goalkeeper is under pressure from attackers or at full stretch, it is not safe to catch the ball. Even then, goalkeepers still control where the ball goes — by deflecting it for a corner kick or by punching it clear.

It is important to remember that the goalkeeper can handle the ball *anywhere in the penalty area*. Goalkeepers prepared to act as extra defenders can learn ways of intercepting passes a long way from goal.

CATCHING HIGH BALLS

Catching high balls, like heading, relies as much on good footwork as good aerial skills. Some goalkeepers run 10 yards to catch or punch crosses from the wing. Try to catch the ball at a comfortable overhead height while adhering to the basic principles:

- one foot take-off;
- head steady and eyes on the ball;
- hands to the side and behind the ball;
- fingers spread and relaxed;
- pull the ball to your chest.

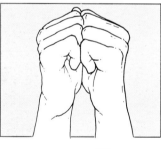

PUNCHING THE BALL

It is important to have a clear idea of where you want to punch the ball. As a general rule, it will be safer to punch the ball out to a wing rather than down the middle of the field. A two-handed punch is preferable, but crosses from the wing may be dealt with by a one-handed overarm punch, knocking the ball towards the opposite wing from which the cross came.

DEFLECTING THE BALL

When deflecting a shot or center, goalkeepers use their fingers or the palm of the hand. Be prepared to stretch your arm and fingertips if the shot requires a full-length dive or a jump at an angle. It will usually be safer to deflect the ball past the goalpost or over the crossbar rather than keeping it in the field of play.

CATCHING A HIGH BALL
United Arab Emirates' goalkeeper Mushin Musabah catches a high ball to stop an attack by Saudi Arabia forwards. Musabah's teammates, having heard his warning call, were aware their goalkeeper was coming for the ball. They have taken up covering positions or, like the defender in the picture (in white), have avoided heading the ball.

 STAR
TIP
When practicing, try to develop an intuition for where your goal is. If you can judge whether a shot is going wide or is on target, that will help you decide whether you will attempt a deflection or let it go over the goal line for a goal kick. It will also help you take a mid-goal position when advancing to narrow the angle (see page 37).

GOALKEEPING (3)

Dino Zoff helped Italy win the 1982 World Cup when he was 40 years old. Peter Shilton (England) and Pat Jennings (Northern Ireland) have also kept goal at the highest level past their fortieth birthday. What helps goalkeepers survive to a relatively late age in international soccer is their positional experience and ability to read the direction of the game. They are quick to spot danger and confident enough to organize defenders into the best positions to relieve that danger.

In their role as extra defender, they sometimes find themselves running out of their penalty area to stop an attack which is building up. In recent years, some goalkeepers have even taken central free kicks *outside* the penalty area, perhaps 30 yards (27m) from the goal being defended. This tactic needs confidence, and is not recommended for nonprofessionals.

SHOUTING INSTRUCTIONS
England goalkeeper Peter Shilton, one of the game's great communicators on the field, shouts instructions to his defenders, warning them of possible dangers. Shilton takes advantage of his experience in reading the pattern of the play and predicting what will develop. The goalkeeper has a view of the whole field.

 STAR TIP
When faced with a one-against-one situation — goalkeeper against lone attacker — advance and take up the "starting position" (see page 32) but wait for him to make a move. Don't commit yourself by diving or falling down, which will help your opponent. If he does shoot, dive sideways rather than feet first to spread yourself across the goal.

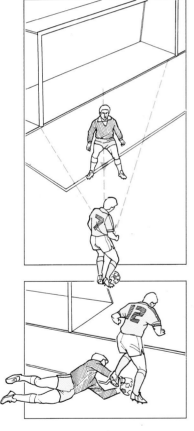

NARROWING THE ANGLE

The more a goalkeeper can advance towards an attacking player, the less unguarded space there is for the player to shoot at. This technique of moving towards the attacker is called "narrowing the angle." The key things to remember are:

- move into the line between the ball and the center of your goal;
- move quickly towards the opponent when he has kicked the ball ahead;
- check and move into a ready position as the attacker reaches the ball;
- advance again if the ball is kicked ahead. If you move too close to the kicker, the ball may be played over your head or taken round you.

DIVING AT FEET

One step further on from narrowing the angle is the ability to dive at a forward's feet, smothering the ball. When making the dive, try to put your body behind the ball, preferably protecting yourself with your upper forearm. The aim, yet again, is to clutch the ball to your chest.

COMMUNICATION

The goalkeeper is in charge of defending the goal. Tell your defense how many you would like in a wall to defend a free kick. Tell them if they are in your way when a corner kick is coming across. Shout "Keeper" when you come for the ball.

GOALKEEPING (4)

1

2

1 DEFENSIVE VOLLEY

Goalkeepers are not only the last line of defense, but also the first line of attack. They must remember the principles of team play – never waste a pass, never give the ball away – and recognize that they can also throw the ball. One common technique for gaining height and distance is the defensive volley. (The volley is explained on page 15.) Set this up by letting the ball *drop* from your hands, rather than throwing it in the air, to prevent an interception.

2 HALF-VOLLEY

The second key kicking technique for a goalkeeper is the half-volley. Here the goalkeeper drops the ball, as for the defensive volley, but strikes it *just after it hits the ground*, the non-kicking foot placed nearer to the ball than for the volley. By striking through the middle of the ball, the pass should be lower and faster than a volleyed clearance. The half-volley, however, is not the best technique for wet or muddy surfaces!

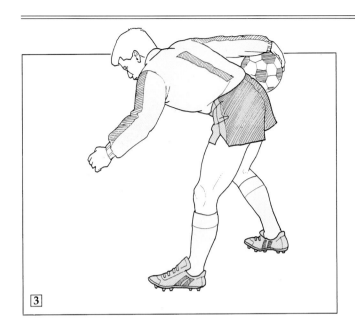

3 ROLLING/BOWLING THE BALL (1)
If a player is unmarked and within 20 yards (18m) of the goalkeeper, then a quick roll of the ball should enable it to reach the target with speed and accuracy. If the goalkeeper is breaking up an attack from one wing, he should look immediately to the other wing. Opponents may have moved across and left a space. The goalkeeper's teammates can help, of course, by looking for the quick throw as soon as the ball is taken.

4 ROLLING/BOWLING THE BALL (2)
The rolling action is similar to that of bowling. One foot should be well in front of the other and the ball released when the hand is level with the front foot. This is a good technique for accuracy but may be dangerous if the ground is muddy or if there are players between the goalkeeper and his teammate. If there is a chance of interception, then the shoulder and overarm throws will be a safer method.

5 THROW FROM THE SHOULDER
One quick distribution technique for distances up to 35 yards (32m) is the throw from the shoulder, the body sideways to, and in line with the target. The ball is released with the head held steady and eyes on the target. Goalkeepers can use their privileged view of the field to put their own team into attack quickly. Like all players, they should have a vision of their passing options as soon as they receive the ball.

6 OVERARM THROW
The overarm throw is the best technique for longer throws of 30 to 40 yards (27-36m). If no opponents are in the way, the throw can be low. If opponents are in the way, the ball can be thrown over them. The key factors are:
- wrap fingers, palm and wrist around the ball;
- body sideways to, and in line with the target;
- legs wide apart for balance;
- move the nonthrowing arm in a downward arc and the throwing arm (kept straight) in an upward arc.

DEFENDING (1)

When the opposition has the ball, everyone in your team has some responsibility to try to win it back.

Defending skills, like heading skills, are often neglected in the young. Even some international stars have poor technique where defending is concerned. Simple points, like forcing an opponent onto his weaker foot, should not be ignored.

If you defend well you will win the ball back more quickly and have a greater chance to attack. The tips below will help you become a better defender, no matter what position you play. They are basic techniques to prevent the opposition moving forward. In certain situations you may also need tackling skills.

STOPPING OPPONENTS TURNING

If your opponent receives the ball with his back to your goal, you can stop him turning by doing four things:

- keep your eye on the ball;
- as the ball reaches your opponent, you should move to within 2 or 3ft (60-90cm) – no closer, or your view may be blocked;
- be patient and stay on your feet – your opponent is in trouble, not you;
- tackle when your opponent either makes a mistake or tries to turn.

If you tackle before this, you will probably commit a foul.

STOPPING THE FORWARD PASS

If your opponent is already facing your goal, you should try to stop him passing the ball forward:

- as the ball travels to him, move quickly to get within 4 to 6ft (1.2–1.8m);
- as soon as he has the ball under control, approach more slowly to keep your balance;
- get into line between the ball and your goal;
- watch the ball closely and react to its movement;
- be patient and stay on your feet.

FORCING OPPONENTS ONE WAY

If you are near the touch line, you can make your opponent go that way to restrict his room to dribble or pass. This is especially useful if you have a teammate covering behind you. Position yourself so your opponent can't go inside.

KEEPING YOUR DISTANCE
Frank Stapleton of the Republic of Ireland (Eire) can probably feel Alberto Gorrez of Spain breathing down his neck, but Gorrez is too close to his opponent, risking conceding a free kick and unable to see the ball. Better technique is shown by England's Kenny Sansom (INSET) as he retains his balance and steers Scotland's Mo Johnston towards the touch line.

 STAR TIP

Commit yourself to a challenge for the ball only when you feel sure you will win it. A good time to try is when you have a teammate covering behind you. In this situation, if your challenge doesn't come off, then you have not risked putting your team in a more dangerous position.

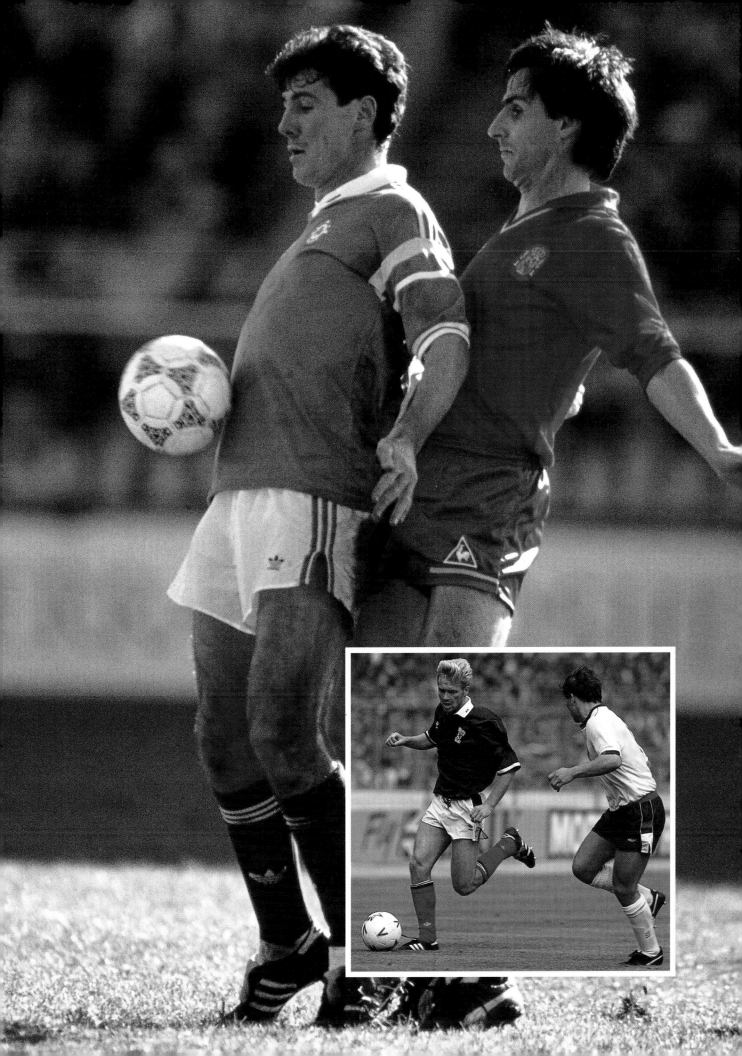

DEFENDING (2)

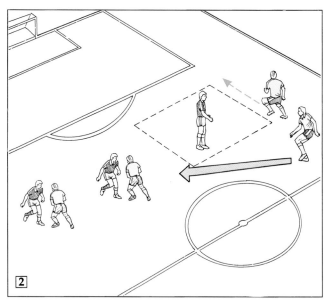

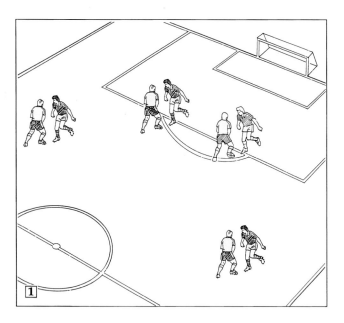

1 ONE-TO-ONE MARKING
When you have mastered some of the basic principles of defending (page 40), it is important to consider your defensive role *as part of a team*. The most common marking system is one-to-one marking, which assigns each player to one specific opponent. When the opposition has the ball, you should know which player you are most responsible for.

2 ZONAL MARKING
Zonal marking is the major alternative to one-to-one marking. Here players are responsible for marking whoever comes into their zone of the field. Whereas a one-to-one defender follows an opponent all around the field, here he hands over responsibility if the opponent crosses to the next zone. Zonal systems usually mean there is less defensive running, but they are complex to organize and are used more often at higher levels of play.

3 SWEEPER SYSTEM
A variation of the one-to-one system, or the zonal system, is the sweeper system. Here one player takes the role of sweeper, playing behind the back line of the defense. The sweeper is not allocated a particular player to mark (if the team is playing one-to-one) or a particular zone (if zonal marking is being played). Instead, the sweeper has a roving role, covering all the defenders, "sweeping up" any mistakes or attacking breakthroughs.

4

5

4 MARKING TIGHTLY

When the opposition has the ball, your defensive action should be determined by *where* the ball is. You should take one of three actions — mark *your* opponent tightly, drop away to cover a colleague, or drop well away from your opponent to give your team balance. Here the first of these actions applies. Your opponent has the ball so you move in and follow the techniques learned on page 40. The closer you are to the ball, the more tightly you should mark.

5 DROPPING AWAY

When you are further away from the ball, your role is to drop away from your opponent and cover a colleague who is now moving in to mark closely. Try to take up a position close enough to support your colleague, ready to move in to challenge if your colleague is beaten. At the same time, you should be able to move up and mark your own opponent if the ball is passed that way.

6 BALANCE IN DEFENSE

When the ball is still further away and there is little chance that someone will send a long pass to the player you are marking, your role is to take a position that gives your defense better balance. Here the defender has moved further around to cover teammates and to cover space into which the ball might be kicked. He will still be able to mark the opponent if the ball is played to him.

6

TEAM TACTICS (1)

Soccer is a team game. There is a time for individualism, of course, but only if it benefits your team. It is little use trying an optimistic shot from an acute angle if an unmarked colleague is waiting for a pass in front of goal. Similarly, it is sensible to concede a corner kick rather than risk a fancy trick in front of your own goal.

No matter what position you are playing, regardless of the number on the shirt you are wearing, you should be playing in the way that suits your team in the situation at the time. If your team is losing 1-0 late in the game, everyone should be concerned with scoring an equalizer without sacrificing your system of play. You should keep each other informed of tactics and do your best to maintain good team spirit and dressing-room harmony. A well-blended team usually holds an advantage over 11 individuals.

A SYSTEM OF PLAY

You should decide on a system of play which suits the players you have available. (The 4-2-4, 4-3-3 and 4-4-2 systems are explained on pages 46 and 47.) Your system should emphasize players' strengths and disguise their weaknesses.

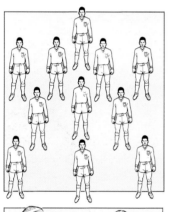

THE CAPTAIN'S ROLE

The captain is the coach's agent *on the field*. He will toss a coin with the opposing captain to decide choice of ends. Toss-winning captains usually prefer to play with the wind behind them and/or any low sun at their backs. The captain will also take responsibility to change tactics if necessary, encourage teammates and point out the responsibilities of other players. If a player is injured or substituted, the captain should ensure all positions are still covered. Captains lead by encouragement, example or as a driving-force. The best combine all three.

THE PENALTY TAKER

A team should take the field knowing who will take the penalty kicks. It should choose a confident, decisive player with good kicking skills who looks forward to a free crack at goal no matter what the pressure. It helps to name a reserve penalty taker in case the first is injured or substituted, or in case the team is awarded two penalties and the original taker would like to decline taking the second.

 STAR TIP

Even though your team should have a system of play, you should not let it detract from your responsibility as an individual. To make sure that you don't let down your teammates, keep practicing your individual skills, such as passing, dribbling, turning, shooting and defending.

TEAM TACTICS (2)

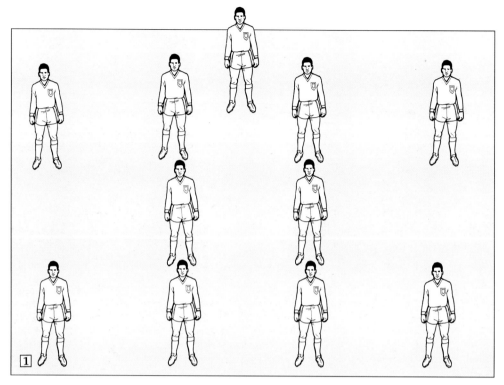

1 THE 4-2-4 SYSTEM
As was stressed on page 44, the system of play you choose should suit the strengths of your players. But no matter what system of play you adopt, it will not be effective unless you have good players. If you have two fast attacking wingers and the players to make long passes to the front runners, then 4-2-4 may work for you. This relies on only two midfield players, suggesting that they may be bypassed some of the time by the long-passing game.

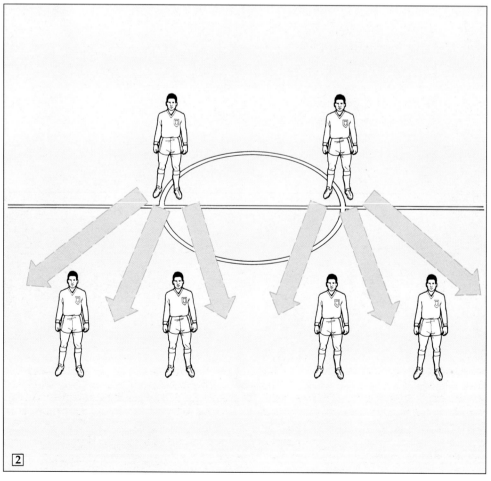

2 The idea of the 4-2-4 system is that you are assured of at least six players defending when the opposition has the ball, and you also have at least six players attacking when your team is in possession. The two midfield players can pull back into a defensive role or support the attackers (as shown in this illustration), depending on what is best for the team.

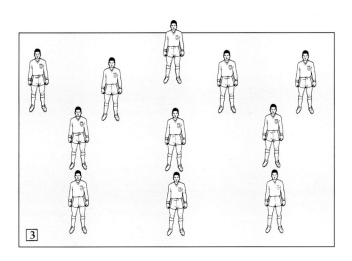

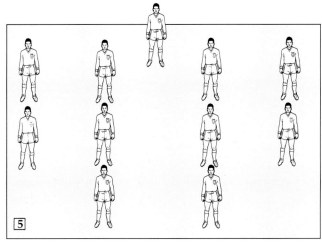

3 THE 4-3-3 SYSTEM

The 4-3-3 system works in a similar fashion to the 4-2-4 system, except that it offers at least seven defensive players and six attacking players, depending on which team has the ball. A variation of this system, to give even more defensive depth, can be made by switching to five defenders and two attackers (a 5-3-2 system), possibly pulling out one of the five defenders into the sweeper role described on page 42.

5 THE 4-4-2 SYSTEM

If your team is overladen with midfield players and defenders, then 4-4-2 can be a useful system. This converts into an apparently strong defensive formation with at least eight players who can go quickly behind the ball if the opposition has possession. This system is also flexible enough to provide an attacking force.

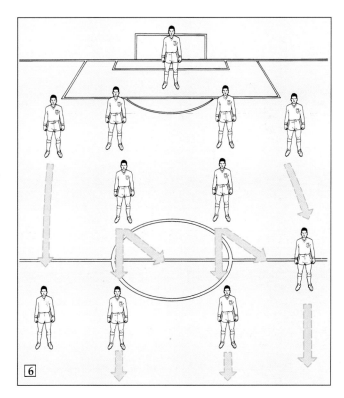

4 The 4-3-3 system may be a better way of distributing the mid-field workload than 4-2-4, especially if your team prefers to build up with shorter passes. When your team does go forward, the three midfield players can come with late runs which may cause more danger for the opposition, as illustrated here.

6 A 4-4-2 system will work only if you have two strong front-runners with good ball control, who are capable of holding the ball when under pressure. The space created by the front-runners can be exploited by the midfield players or even by the wide defenders, who can make overlapping runs (see page 51).

TACTICAL PASSING

Once you have mastered basic techniques of passing (see pages 10 to 15), it is important to understand ways you can improve the quality of your passing in a game. No matter how good your passing technique, if the quality of your passing is poor, your technique will not be effective. Accuracy is only one necessary quality. Other considerations are explained below.

Soccer is a simple game — providing you pass well and keep possession of the ball. In this way, the ball covers the ground rather than your legs. You are letting the ball do the work. When watching star players, notice how little they give the ball to an opponent. If you have any soccer ambitions, work on all aspects of your passing. Remember not to pass the ball to teammates who are likely to be in more trouble with the ball than you are. Look for players who are better placed than you.

PASSING BACK

Try to pass forward if you can, to reduce the number of opponents between the ball and the goal. Sometimes, though, it is safer to go back first. An example is a tightly marked defender facing his own goal. A goalkeeper can help by coming out to take a pass back but all players can support teammates (see pages 50 and 51).

THE WALL PASS

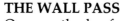

One method of temporarily excluding opponents from the game is the wall pass. A teammate acts like a wall, rebounding your original pass into a better position. This can be used in two-on-two or two-on-one situations. You pass quickly to your teammate, then immediately run into a better position to receive the return. Your opponent has the disadvantage of having to turn.

HELPING THE RECEIVER

Besides accuracy, good passing needs correct weighting, timing and sometimes disguise. The *weighting* is how hard you kick the ball. Overweighted passes will be too difficult to control or will run out of play. Soft passes will be intercepted. The *timing* is when you kick it. If you delay, the pass may be blocked or your teammate may be offside. If you pass too early, the ball may run out of play. As for *disguise*, the less obviously you make your pass, the less chance there is of interception.

KEEP THINKING
This superb action shot of the Brazilian Branco emphasizes the power of thinking at international level. With the ball in his control, Branco steals a very quick glance at the rest of the field, ready to decide what he should do next to gain the maximum effect.

 STAR TIP
Try to be aware of the positions of opponents and teammates by looking around the field, even before you receive the ball. By doing this, good players know what they are going to do with the ball as soon as they receive it. Good players do not play with their heads down. They play with "vision," which means constantly checking where everyone is.

RUNNING OFF THE BALL

Nothing better demonstrates that soccer is a team game than players running into positions to support a teammate who has possession of the ball. The message is simple: when your team is in possession, get into position.

Of course, this is easier said than done. In a winning team, every player will be wanting the ball. In a losing team, players may not be so keen, yet that is the time when it is even more important to keep running.

Your main aim when running into position is to give the player with the ball an extra option. Sometimes that option may not be used and your colleague may pass to another player, shoot for goal or dribble the ball. Whatever happens, make sure you continue to offer your running off the ball to help create space and provide support.

GIVING THE GREEN LIGHT
Olaf Thon of West Germany gives the green light for players to make a run off the ball.
INSET: As Thon (white shirt) is challenged by Republic of Ireland (Eire) defenders, two West German players in the background are trying to find supporting positions to help him. The more you play with your colleagues, the more you will know what kind of runs they would like from you.

 STAR TIP
If a teammate has the ball under control and has some time and space, he will probably raise his head to view the other players' positions. That look should be a green light for you to make your forward run to receive the ball. If your teamwork is good, your teammate will know where you are going. His quick look has acted as a signal to you.

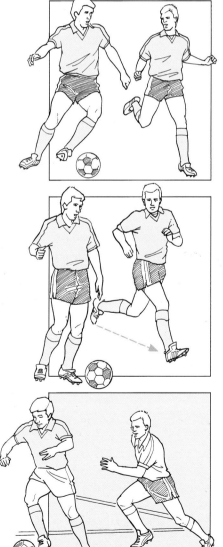

CALLING

Calling is an important part of the game. Call clearly, using a name, e.g. "My ball, Gary," "Yours, Jim." If you are watching a game, listen to the players as well. Try to develop the ability to recognize when your teammates are in good positions, because calling also alerts your opponents. Try to warn a teammate if an opponent is closing him down on his blind side.

PROVIDING SUPPORT

You can provide support either behind your colleague or in front. Support behind if your teammate is tightly marked and must play the ball back. Run to a position 10 yards (9m) from him, at an angle of 45 degrees. Support in front when your teammate has the time and space to play the pass forward. One of the best angles is provided by a player escaping his marker and making an overlap run, outside his teammate, to receive a pass on the move.

CREATING SPACE

If you are being marked well, when you get the ball your opponent will be a yard or two behind. It is important to use deception strategies to increase that distance, giving yourself enough space to receive a pass and perhaps turn. A simple strategy is to pretend to run one way and, after a stride or two, to sprint in another direction, wrong-footing your marker. Your speed off the mark is again important.

Set Plays (1)

During a soccer game the ball is out of play almost as much as it is in play. It makes sense, therefore, to work on ways of restarting play that may gain your team an advantage. In fact, about half of all goals follow a set play, but more at the higher levels of soccer. This level of success can only come by *rehearsing* moves.

Set plays, sometimes called "set pieces," include goal kicks, throw-ins, corner kicks, free kicks and place kicks. They will occur in all games, which means there can be swift reward for practicing set-piece play in training.

Some examples of possible moves are shown on the following pages, but try to choose moves which suit your players. It is little use chipping corner kicks or free kicks into the penalty area if you have no good headers of the ball.

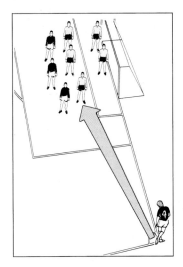

THROW-INS

Taking a throw-in is an art, and should fall to three or four players in your team who have practiced. To avoid a foul throw, study the wording of soccer's Law 15: "The thrower at the moment of delivering the ball must face the field of play and part of each foot shall be either on the touch line or on the ground outside the touch line. The thrower shall use both hands and shall deliver the ball from behind and over his head."

FREE KICKS

Free kicks can occur anywhere on the field. First check whether the kick is direct, from which a goal can be scored without touching another player. The referee should signal with one arm raised high in the air if the kick is indirect. If in doubt, check with the referee. Then use the opportunity to put your team in a better position, perhaps using one of the moves shown on page 54.

CORNER KICKS

Corner kicks are an excellent attacking opportunity. They can be played to the near or far post, or short-range (see page 55). A corner-kick specialist should be a strong, accurate striker of a stationary ball. He should keep his teammates informed of what he intends to do with the kick. The worst move would be to put it behind the goal line for a goal kick.

TAKING A FREE KICK
Carlos Valdarrama of Colombia waits to take a free kick in a World Cup qualifying game. He is either asking the referee to move back an opponent who is within 10 yards (9m) or he is giving a signal to teammates.
INSET: West German players acclaim a well-worked free kick which has resulted in a goal by Andreas Brehme against Italy.

 STAR
TIP

Try to keep set plays fairly simple if you can. The more players involved, the more likely it is that something will go wrong. If only two or three players are involved, there is a greater chance that they can practice together and develop a set of signals. More than three will probably be too many. Keep it simple, make it slick.

SET PLAYS (2)

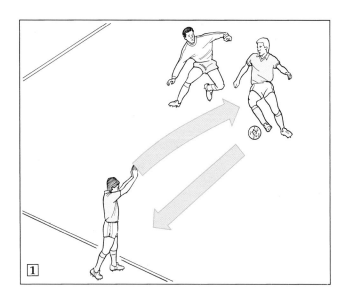

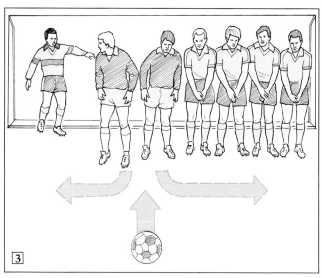

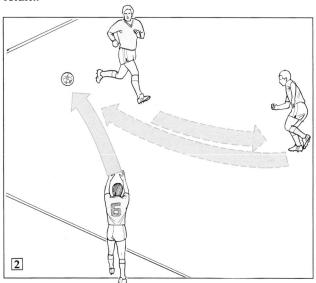

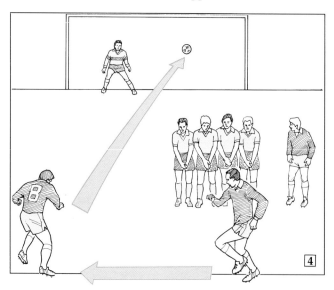

1 THROW-IN

The person taking the throw-in is often unmarked. From this position, advantage can be gained by the simple tactic of passing the ball back to the thrower. A teammate should take a position about 10 yards (9m) from the thrower, creating a little extra space by wrong-footing his marker (see page 51). A throw to his feet will allow him to pass back to the thrower, who should step onto the field of play before receiving the return.

3 DIRECT FREE KICKS

At direct free kicks just outside the penalty area, a stationary ball should be easier to strike than a moving ball, but the opposition may have formed a wall of players. Block the goalkeeper's view with two players on the end of the wall. They should be 1 yard (90cm) nearer to the kicker than the wall, so that they can run away just as the kicker has his head down and his foot back to shoot at them. One runs across the front of the wall, the other in the opposite direction.

2 THROW-IN: SECOND OPTION

A second throw-in uses the cross-over tactic. The thrower's two teammates interchange positions. The players marking them face a difficult decision when they cross over. They may hesitate or even bump into each other. That is the time to throw the ball. A throw forward into space should be to the advantage of the thrower's team. The throw should be downwards, so that the ball bounces a few times before it reaches the moving teammate, making it easier to control.

4 DIRECT FREE KICKS: SECOND OPTION

A second option is to play the free kick across for another player to shoot for the open side of the goal. A player stationed on the other end of the wall — he should take care to stay onside — is useful in case there is a rebound from the goalkeeper. Make sure someone follows up all shots from free kicks.

5 CORNER KICKS

A common corner kick tactic is the near-post corner for a flick-on header. The corner-kick taker should swing the ball in, right-footed from the left wing or left-footed from the right. The target is the corner of the six-yard area, and one attacker's job is to arrive there and deflect a header backwards (see page 20). Three players make separate runs into the goal area, so one of them can head the ball into the net whatever the strength of the back-header.

5

6 SHORT CORNERS

If you are not happy with a stationary ball at a corner kick, and would prefer to kick a moving ball, then a well-worked short corner will provide that chance. A player comes away from the six-yard area, running down the goal line. He takes the pass and returns it at a 45-degree angle. The corner-kick taker, having run across, is now in a position to make a cross from shorter range or perhaps even try a shot.

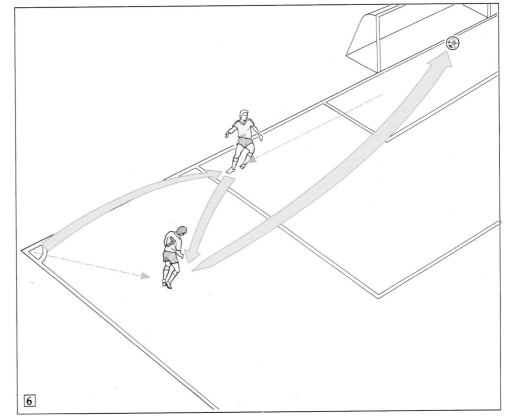

6

PENALTY KICKS

Penalty kicks are tense two-person duels which affect results of games more than other incidents.

Take the case of Brazil in the 1986 World Cup Finals. Brazil failed to progress to the semifinal of the competition because of three penalty misses. Near the end of the game against France, Zico missed a penalty with the score 1-1. Then two other Brazilians missed in the penalty kick shoot-out.

During a game, penalty kicks are awarded for any foul that merits a direct free kick which is committed by the defending team in the penalty area. This includes fouls for kicking, tripping, jumping, violent charging, striking, holding, pushing or handling the ball.

The penalty-kick taker is alone with the goalkeeper, and both must decide what to do. A change of mind, or a change of heart, will almost certainly mean failure. Whether taking or facing a kick, choose your strategy and be positive about it.

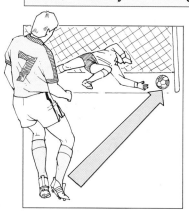

PLACING THE SHOT
Whatever method of penalty-taking you use — whether placing the ball away from the goalkeeper or blasting the ball — you should have first mastered basic kicking techniques (see pages 10-15). Placing a ball is simply passing the ball into goal. Choose your spot and shoot for that spot whatever happens.

HITTING THE BALL HARD
Striking the ball with good shooting technique is crucial (see page 31). The hard-hit penalty relies more on power than accuracy, but remember that goalkeepers will have more chance to save a waist-high shot, so keep your body over the ball and strike it low.

FACING A PENALTY KICK
Just as the penalty-kick taker needs to be clear about what to do, so must the goalkeeper. Two strategies are available:
- try to guess where the penalty taker will kick the ball, and dive and spread yourself in that general area;
- wait until just before the ball is struck, when you should be able to tell where it is going, and *then* make a good save. With a lot of penalties at junior level, the ball crosses the line close to the goalkeeper, so the second strategy is probably better.

PENALTY–KICK PRESSURE
Pressure can affect the very best of players. In the 1988 European Championship Final, the Soviet Union was awarded a penalty kick when 2-0 down to Holland. Igor Belanov tries to place his kick but shoots weakly. Dutch goalkeeper Hans Van Breukelen, who had conceded the penalty, dives slightly to his right to make a textbook save.

 STAR TIP
If you are taking a penalty kick, boost your confidence by reminding yourself of your advantages. Whereas you know what you are going to do with the penalty, the goalkeeper has to guess. You can take a run-up to the ball but the goalkeeper must stay on the goal line and cannot move either foot until the ball has been kicked.

ACTION STUDY

In the post-war era, there has never been a greater favorite to win the English F.A. Cup Final than Liverpool in 1988. Liverpool had dominated the decade and, having already sealed the 1987-88 League Championship (for a record seventeenth time), expected to lift yet another trophy.

Liverpool's Cup Final opposition, Wimbledon, had no soccer pedigree. Eleven years previously they were in the Southern League, not even among the top 92 clubs in the country. Their success, which included a rise from the Fourth to the First Division in three years, had been based on a direct style of soccer and an approach which some would call aggressive and others brutal. Wimbledon's disciplinary record was not good, but the team had the capacity to work hard and play for each other. In 1988 they were coached by Don Howe.

Wimbledon used a 4-2-4 system which relied on long (and often high) passes for their aggressive forwards, frequently bypassing the two midfield players. In contrast, Liverpool preferred a patient possession game which had a long-proven record of success. Liverpool players had wonderful individual skills and blended into a flexible unit. John Barnes, voted player of the year by journalists and players in 1988, and John Aldridge were both scoring goals regularly.

We have chosen to feature two incidents from that Cup Final to show the speed of thinking and acting in high-level soccer. Liverpool has had much more success than Wimbledon, but the 1988 F.A. Cup Final is a reminder that a confident, well-organized team can beat the strongest of favorites if it can get its technique and psychology right on the big day.

[1] Wimbledon's Lawrie Sanchez (blue shirt, center) shows that the secret of attacking heading is running to the right place. He deflects Dennis Wise's free kick, taken from near the corner flag.

[2] The referee is perfectly positioned to watch. But four Liverpool defenders and goalkeeper Bruce Grobbelaar can only watch too. Sanchez (hidden by post) turns to see the outcome of his header.

[3] As there is no defender covering the post, the ball drops neatly into the net, to the delight of the two Wimbledon players, whose anticipation has proved more important than weight of numbers.

4 Anticipation is also crucial in this second incident after an hour of the game. Wimbledon goalkeeper and captain Dave Beasant dives to his left to beat away John Aldridge's penalty.

5 Wimbledon players congratulate Beasant. It was obvious to players of both sides that this was an important save. Liverpool's job was to try to raise their game once more; the Wimbledon players had the job of retaining their concentration and their lead.

6 Liverpool's Australian star Craig Johnston makes an incredible jump to bring his team back into the game. The psychological blow of the penalty save affected the Liverpool team badly, although Johnston, who had come on as substitute, continued to try to lift his team by a typically spirited display.

MENTAL APPROACH

Soccer is an emotional game. It can bring tension, anger, joy, despair and elation. Part of knowing about soccer is being able to deal with your feelings in a way that will help your team.

Before the game you may feel nervous. International stars expect to be nervous, but they know their nerves will settle when they start kicking a ball. If you are not nervous, it may be a sign that you are not taking the game seriously or have not prepared particularly well.

Try to find your own way to deal with pregame nerves. Some players develop superstitions, such as wearing the same clothes to each game or coming onto the field after their teammates, and others may use relaxation exercises or deep breathing to settle the tension. Humor helps, and a comic character in the dressing room may help to settle down some players.

Part of the role of the coach or manager is to relax the players before the kick-off. You should be reminded of the preparation you have done, and be reassured that you are well prepared.

On the field, though, you are your own boss. You will probably hear the shouts from the touch line, but the final decisions are yours, taking heed of your captain. Soccer needs thought. What can be changed? What can I do to gain the upper hand over the opposition?

Try to support your teammates rather than criticize them, and, above all, respect the decision of the referee. Getting angry or disputing a decision won't help your team, especially if you receive a caution for dissent or are sent off.

1 PLAYER-COACH RELATIONSHIP
The relationship between the players and the coach is very important in determining the success of the team. Bilardo (left) and Maradona of Argentina are photographed during the 1986 World Cup competition, won by Argentina.

2 NERVES
Tense faces and hardly a smile among them. England players nurse their pregame nerves as they await the start of a World Cup qualifying game.

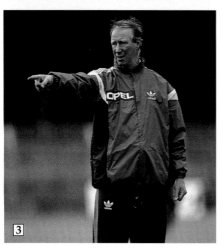

3 PSYCHOLOGY
A coach will use psychology to get the best from players. Jack Charlton, a World Cup winner with England in 1966, coached the Republic of Ireland (Eire) into the 1988 European Championship Finals and the 1990 World Cup Finals. Eire is one of the smallest nations in Europe with less than 4 million inhabitants.

4 IS IT ALL IN THE MIND?
John Harkes of the United States ponders his next move.

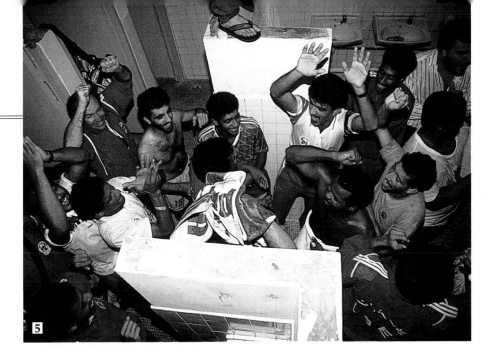

5 HAPPY PLAYERS
Dressing-room harmony is important to success. The happy players here are the United Arab Emirates, after qualifying for the 1990 World Cup Finals.

6 SUPPORTERS
Support helps, and these Cameroon fans leave no doubt about their allegiance.

7 VICTORY
Finally, there may be the joy of victory – celebrations on the United States' team bench after qualification for the 1990 World Cup Finals.

THE ROLE OF OFFICIALS

The game of soccer survives because many people are willing to devote time and energy to work behind the scenes. In the majority of cases this work is unpaid.

First there is the playing field. A groundsman is employed to take care of its surface and line markings. Other staff need to ensure that medical treatment is available in an emergency. An organizer, or secretary, is required, to liaise with opponents and/or the league. A coach or manager is needed to choose the team, and give it a clear strategy. And, during the game, there are the referee and two linesmen, who play key roles and are probably the only three neutral people at the game.

At a professional level, a soccer club needs even more staff than this to survive — scouts to recruit players, financial advisers, fundraisers, publicists, groundstaff, physiotherapists, program sellers — the list is endless.

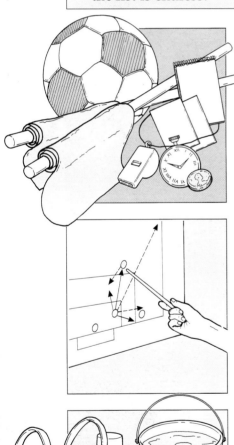

REFEREES AND LINESMEN

A referee acts as a timekeeper and enforces the laws on the field of play. A referee is supported by two linesmen, who each patrol a half of the touch line on opposite sides of the field. The linesmen indicate throw-ins, offsides and infringements to the referee, but the referee's decision is final.

MANAGERS AND COACHES

Managers and coaches can have stressful roles, frustrated at the sidelines as they watch their players. Before a game, a coach can devise tactics, deal in sport psychology and work on individual skills. During a game, positional changes and substitutions can be made, but the rest is up to the players.

TRAINER

A trainer (or physiotherapist) will be in charge of a first-aid kit, which may include a bucket of water, a sponge, antiseptic creams, pain-relieving spray, smelling salts, various types of bandage and scissors. In addition, he should make sure that a stretcher and splints are available in case of serious injury. The trainer should also know the location of the nearest telephone, even on unfamiliar grounds. During a game, it is essential that the trainer is present to help give first-aid to injured players.

QUICK THINKING
Referees must make up their minds quickly. They have the final decision on points of fact during the game, even if that decision is unpopular. This is a scene from a World Cup qualifying game between the United Arab Emirates and Saudi Arabia in October 1989. Hassian Shaibani (U.A.E.) is arguing about a disallowed goal. There were no goals scored in the game.

 STAR TIP
Your first concern is the players' safety, not the result. Don't force players with serious injuries to continue. The best cure for impact injuries is not heat treatment but:
REST the injured part for at least 48 hours,
applying crushed ICE,
COMPRESS with a strapping or bandage, and
ELEVATE the affected part of the body. (The acronym for this is RICE.)

FITNESS AND TRAINING (1)

Throughout this book we have stressed the benefit of *practicing* your skills, but other aspects of your game will also need practice. Preparation for playing is as important as the actual playing. Nothing gives a team more confidence than the feeling that they are capable of surviving the whole match without feeling tired and with a few rehearsed tricks up their sleeves. Training as a team is also a good way to build up team spirit and confidence in set-play moves.

There is an old saying that you only get out of the game what you put in. Certainly it is true to say that what you put into training will bring you rewards — if only fewer injuries and less stiffness two days after a game. You will need to develop sensible methods of warming up your body to prevent pulled muscles, and you will need to work on your speed and stamina, although young players should be fit enough with ball work and practice games alone. You should also pay some attention to a sensible diet to maintain good health.

SOLO TRAINING
Paul Caligiuri of the United States is shown running along the seashore. The beach surface is good for building up strength in the leg muscles. If Caligiuri can train on wet, sandy surfaces, he will also be at home on muddy soccer fields.
INSET: Players of the United Arab Emirates are being put through their warm-up routine.

 STAR TIP
Try to arrange training so that there is plenty of ball work, friendly competition and team work. These aspects are likely to retain the players' interests more, and they mirror more closely the events of a real game. Solo running is in no way a replica of team play, although it is better than nothing.

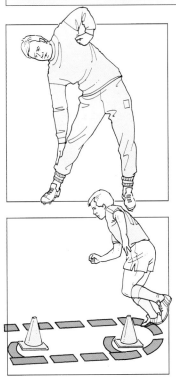

WARMING UP
Soccer demands action from most muscles in the body. You should prepare for the game with a set of exercises which gradually stretch the muscles of your legs (see page 66), arms, neck and torso. Wearing a sweatsuit if the weather is cold, try these exercises in the 10-15 minutes before the game. You may also want to watch what professional players do when they take the field.

SPEED TRAINING
Speed over the first 5 or 10 yards (4.5-9m) is crucial in soccer — to escape defenders or to cover players quickly when defending. Most teams will work on sprinting and turning exercises in training, with or without a ball. Relay races can be organized between two teams, half at each end of a 10-yard (9m) sprint.

STAMINA TRAINING
Stamina is built up through the *amount* of training, ensuring that players do more training than they will need in the game, especially late in the game when pressures are at their greatest. The build-up needs to be gradual, however. Shuttle runs force a player to run 5 yards (4.5m) and back, 10 yards (9m) and back, and so on up to 25 yards (23m).

FITNESS AND TRAINING (2)

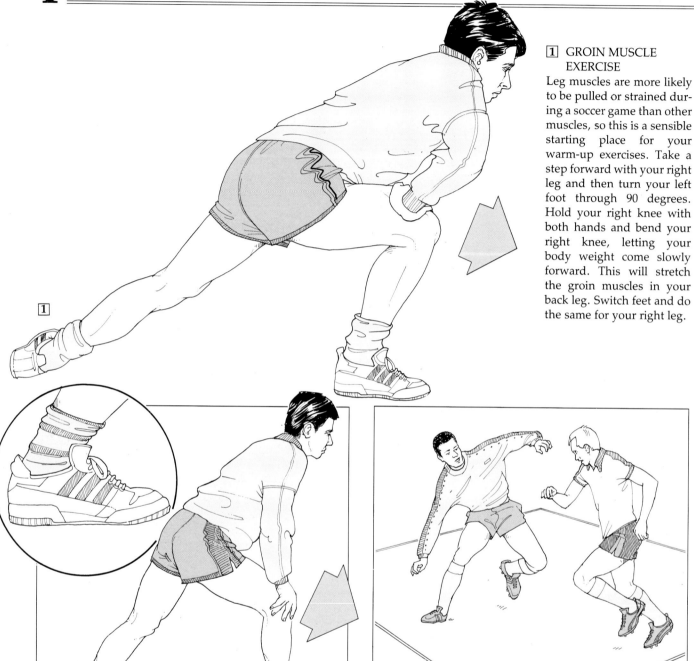

1 GROIN MUSCLE EXERCISE
Leg muscles are more likely to be pulled or strained during a soccer game than other muscles, so this is a sensible starting place for your warm-up exercises. Take a step forward with your right leg and then turn your left foot through 90 degrees. Hold your right knee with both hands and bend your right knee, letting your body weight come slowly forward. This will stretch the groin muscles in your back leg. Switch feet and do the same for your right leg.

2 CALF MUSCLE EXERCISE
This second stretching exercise works on the calf muscles. Again, take one step forward with your right leg, but this time keep your back foot pointing towards the front leg. Keeping your back heel (your left) on the ground, bend the front leg. This will stretch the calf muscle in your left leg. Then put your left foot forward and do the same to stretch the calf muscle in your right leg.

3 "FAKE AND DODGE"
One exercise to improve turning and sprinting over short distances is the "fake and dodge" game. Having marked out a grid in the form of a square, set one person to catch the other without either leaving the square. There should be a time limit, say, 10 seconds. The game is to improve deception techniques, and is usually played without a ball.

4 TURN AND SPRINT
Another good turning-and-sprinting exercise used by coaches involves one player running backwards and another running forwards. The distance between the two players should be 2 or 3 yards (1.8-2.7m). On a signal from the coach, the player running backwards must turn round and out-sprint the other to a marker. This exercise is good training for many situations which will arise during a game.

5 STAMINA
Young players should be able to reach a good level of stamina by playing games and practicing with a ball, but at a later stage of your soccer career you will need to think seriously about your stamina. Shuttle runs are well tested. These can be long or short − 5 yards (4.5m) to a marker, 5 yards (4.5m) back, 10 yards (9m) to the next marker, 10 yards (9m) back, and so on, perhaps up to distances of 100 yards (91.4m).

6 COOPER RUNS
A really testing stamina exercise is that of Cooper runs. Here the players simply run along the outside lines of the field as many times as they can in 12 minutes. As this is a timed exercise, players can monitor their progress.

TESTING YOURSELF

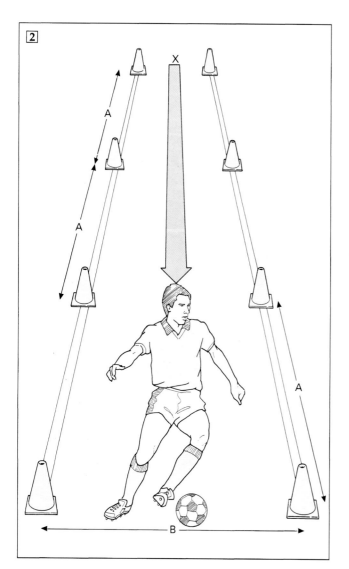

1 TURNING

To practice your *turning* ability, set out a grid which is 5 yards (4.5m) square. Start with the ball on one line of the square, then run over the opposite line and turn to come back. Do this twice, ending by stopping the ball just past the line where you started. This will involve three turns, all of which should be of the same kind (see page 26). Someone should time you with a stopwatch as you practice.

2 RUNNING WITH THE BALL

To test yourself at *running with the ball*, set up two rows of markers at 10-yard (9m) intervals. The rows should be 2 yards (1.8m) apart. Ask someone to time you with a stopwatch as you run with the ball from one end to the other. Within the last 10 yards (9m) you may either pass the ball or run with it to the end, but remember that your passing needs to be accurate to hit a 2-yard (1.8m) space. Try to improve your time on each attempt.

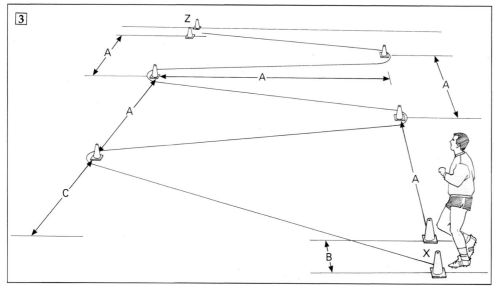

3 SPEED

In order to test your *speed*, organize the markers as shown in the diagram and ask someone to time you as you run around the course. This exercise can take place without a ball. Remember to run around each marker, not over it, and then sprint to the finish. As with all these tests, you should be timed to within a tenth of a second. Take turns at timing each other and try to improve with each attempt.

4 DRIBBLING

For the *dribbling* exercise, the markers are set up in a similar way as for the exercise to test your speed above. The test is to dribble the ball in front of the markers, but over the line between the markers. You should start and finish with one foot on the ball, standing beyond a 2-yard (1.8m) gate at the end of the course. Again, this exercise should also be timed to give you a target to aim at.

KEY
A 10 yards (9m)
B 2 yards (1.8m)
C 5 yards (4.5m)
D 6 yards (5.5m)
E 12 yards (11m)
F 18 yards (16.5m)
G 3 yards (2.7m)
X START
Z FINISH

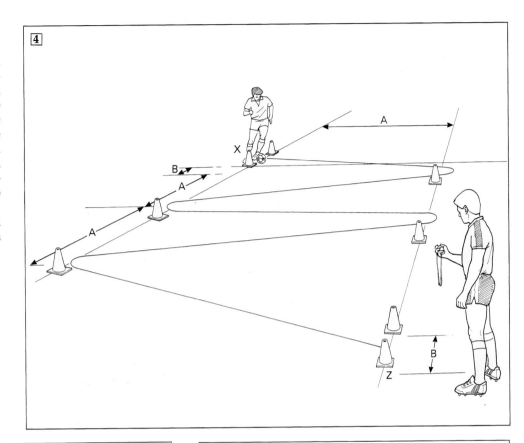

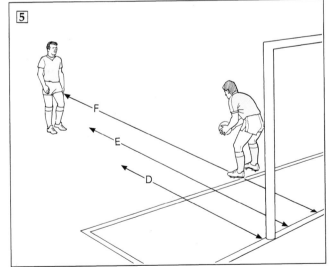

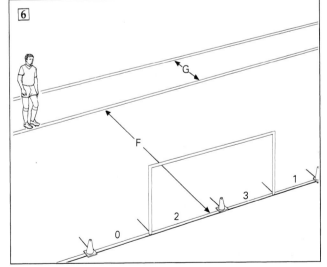

5 HEADING

To test your *heading* ability, start by standing at a reasonable distance from the goal. This can be 6 yards (5.5m), 12 yards (11m) or 18 yards (16.5m), depending on how experienced you are. Ask someone to throw the ball underarm so that it would land a little in front of you if you let it bounce. Instead of letting it bounce, though, head it back towards the goal. If it goes into the goal without bouncing more than once, give yourself a point.

6 SHOOTING

To monitor your *shooting*, set up the field as shown in the diagram. Starting from a position 18 yards (16.5m) from the goal line and level with the near post, touch the ball forward (no more than 3 yards (2.7m)) and shoot while the ball is moving. Aim at the far side of the goal and score your shot depending on where it goes — 3 points if it goes in the far half of the goal, 2 points in the near half and 1 point for a near miss at the far post.

GLOSSARY

Advantage — when the referee decides not to give a free kick to a team because a stoppage would mean the team would lose the advantage they had gained.

Away-goals rule — applies when the scores are level after two legs (home and away) of certain European Cup ties; goals scored by away teams in the tie are deemed to count double.

Back four — the four back defenders who form a line of defense in front of the goal.

Booking — what players call a caution. The player's name and number are noted by the referee who then holds up a yellow card.

Caution — a referee has power to issue a caution, or warning, to players who enter or leave the field of play without the referee's permission, persistently infringe the laws, show dissent to the referee or are guilty of "ungentlemanly conduct."

Center back — one of two or more central defenders.

Center forward — the traditional name for the central striker.

Center half — the central defender.

Chip — a pass made by kicking the bottom of the ball with little follow-through, so the ball gains height rather than distance.

Corner kick — a kick awarded to the attacking team when the ball goes over the goal line and was last touched by a member of the defending team.

Covering — when the opposition is in possession, taking a position behind your teammate in case he is beaten.

Crossbar — the bar, 8ft (2.4m) high, which connects the two goalposts.

Crossover — when two teammates switch positions to confuse the opposition.

Cushion control — when a player stops a moving ball in such a way that the body acts as a cushion and the ball drops to the feet.

Dangerous play — when players raise their feet above waist height in a way that is dangerous to an opponent's head or upper body. The referee will award an indirect free kick.

Defender — a player whose major responsibility is to prevent the other team from scoring rather than assist the attack.

Deflecting — altering the direction of the ball without stopping it.

Drag back — a method of turning with the ball where the player rolls the sole of the shoe over the ball to bring it back towards him.

Dribbling — when an individual uses footwork to take the ball past an opponent.

Dropped ball — when the referee, having stopped the game while the ball was still in play, restarts the game by dropping the ball. Players can touch a dropped ball when it has hit the ground.

Extra time — a spell of extra play, usually 15 minutes each way, to decide a cup tie where the scores are level after 90 minutes.

Far post — the goalpost furthest away from a player who is on the wing.

Firm control — when a player controls the ball so that it is deliberately played into a nearby space for the same player to collect within the next stride or two.

Forward — a more traditional term for a striker, a player who is mainly engaged in making and scoring goals.

Free kick (direct) — a free kick from which a goal can be scored without another player needing to touch the ball.

Free kick (indirect) — a free kick from which the ball needs to touch another player before a goal can be scored.

Fullback — a player operating on either the right or left defense.

Goal area — or six-yard box — is the area nearest the goal from where goal kicks must be taken.

Goal difference — a method of deciding the superior team in a league where teams have finished level on points. Often the method used is to subtract the number of goals conceded from the number of goals scored.

Goal kick — a kick awarded to the defending team when the ball goes over the goal line and was last touched by a member of the attacking team.

Half-volley — when the ball is kicked just after it touches the ground.

Injury time — time added on by the referee to the end of each half to compensate for time lost when players were receiving treatment on the field for injuries. The referee may also add on time to compensate for time-wasting by players.

Jockeying — when a defender retreats between the attacker and the goal, forcing the attacker to go in one particular direction while other defenders recover their positions.

Kickoff — the ritual of starting the game and restarting play after each goal and the half-time interval. The ball must travel forward its circumference from a place kick before it is in play.

Libero — a player who takes the role of sweeper and has the freedom to cover other defenders rather than mark specific opponents.

Marking — taking a position close to an opponent to deny the opponent space if the ball is passed that way.

Midfield player — a player whose major responsibilities are to feed forwards with passes and help the defense, if necessary.

Narrowing the angle — when a goalkeeper advances towards an attacking player and reduces the amount of goal the attacker can shoot at.

Near post – the post nearest to a player who is on the wing.

Offside – players are in an offside position if they are nearer the opponents' goal line than the ball, unless there are at least two opponents nearer the goal line at the time the ball is played. (You cannot be offside when in your own half of the field.) Players are not offside if, in the referee's opinion, they are not interfering with play or gaining advantage, or if they receive the ball directly from a goal kick, corner kick, throw-in or dropped ball.

Overlap – when a player runs outside another to offer a good angle for a pass.

Own-goal – when a goal is scored but the ball was last played by a member of the defending team.

Penalty area – the marked-out area, measuring 18 yards by 44 yards (16.4m by 40.2m), in which the goalkeeper can handle the ball and a penalty kick will be awarded if a defender commits an offense punishable by a direct free kick.

Penalty kick – a direct kick taken 12 yards (10.9m) from the goal's center with all players except the goal-keeper and kicker outside the penalty area and arc.

Penalty shoot-out – a method of deciding a cup tie when the scores are level at the end of extra time. Each team takes five penalties and, if the scores are still

level, then penalties are taken on a sudden-death basis.

Place kick – a kick taken while the ball is stationary in the center of the field and from which the ball must go into the opponents' half.

Push pass – a pass pushed with the inside of the foot over a short distance.

Running off the ball – when a player makes a run in support of a teammate who has the ball.

Sending off – players can be sent from the field of play by the referee if they are, in the referee's opinion, guilty of violent conduct, serious foul play, foul or abusive language, or persistent misconduct after a caution in the same game.

Set play – any rehearsed move to restart play from a throw-in, corner kick or free kick.

Eire celebrate as Michel of Spain scores an own goal. This enabled Eire to qualify for the 1990 World Cup.

Shielding the ball – when a player runs with the ball in such a way that his body is kept between the ball and an opponent, and the ball is kept out of playing distance of the opponent.

Skill – choosing the correct technique and being able to perform it in a game.

Striker – a player whose major responsibility is to make or score goals.

Sweeper – a player who plays behind the other defenders, covering them and tidying up any defensive mistakes or attacking breakthroughs.

Technique – a single soccer action, e.g. a pass or a shot.

Through ball – a positive

pass played beyond a number of opponents for a teammate to run on to for a clear run to goal.

Throw-in – the restarting of play after the ball goes over the touchline, the throw being taken by a member of the team that didn't touch the ball last.

Vision – a player's ability to see the whereabouts of the other players and understand the full range of passing options that are available.

Volley – a ball kicked before it bounces, from either the side or the front, in either attack or defense.

Wall pass – where a player makes a pass and receives an immediate return pass at an angle as the teammate acts like a wall.

Winger – someone who plays on the extreme right or left of the attack.

INDEX